REPEATABLE BACKGROUNDS
Geometric and Abstract Patterns

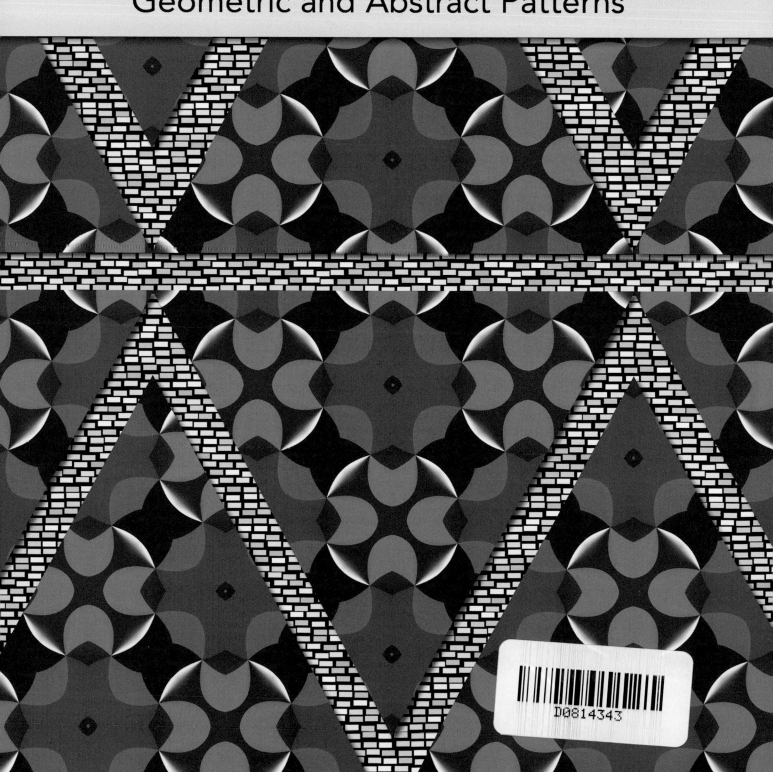

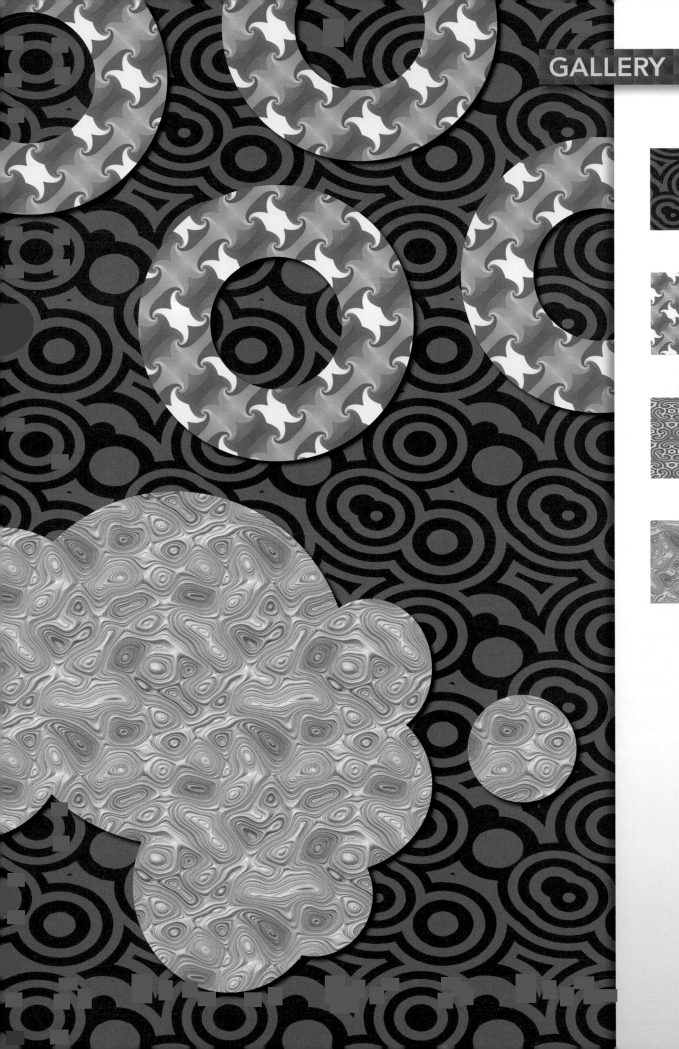

180

132

140

025

147

039

093

174

086

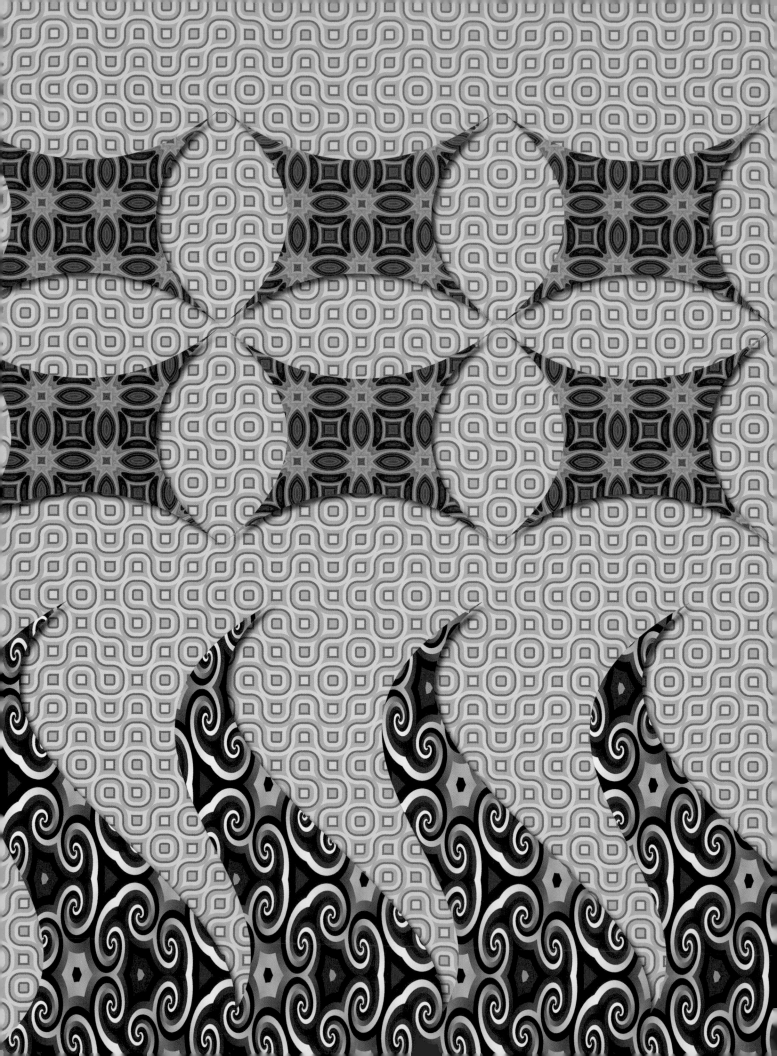

108

137

006

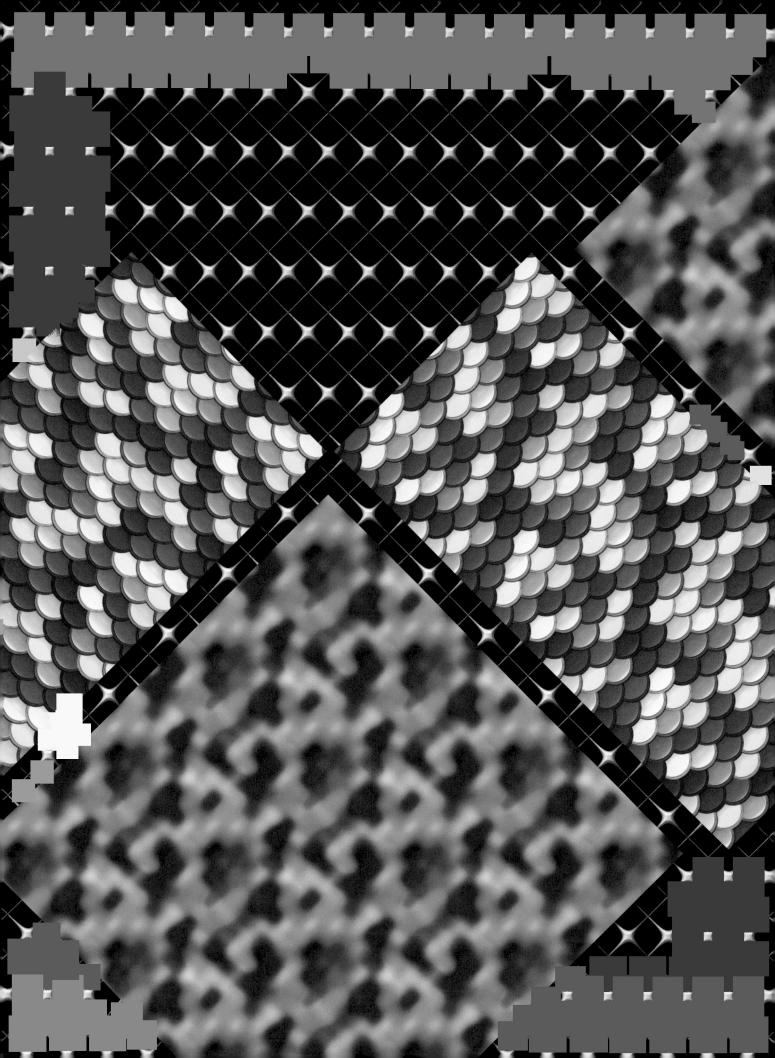

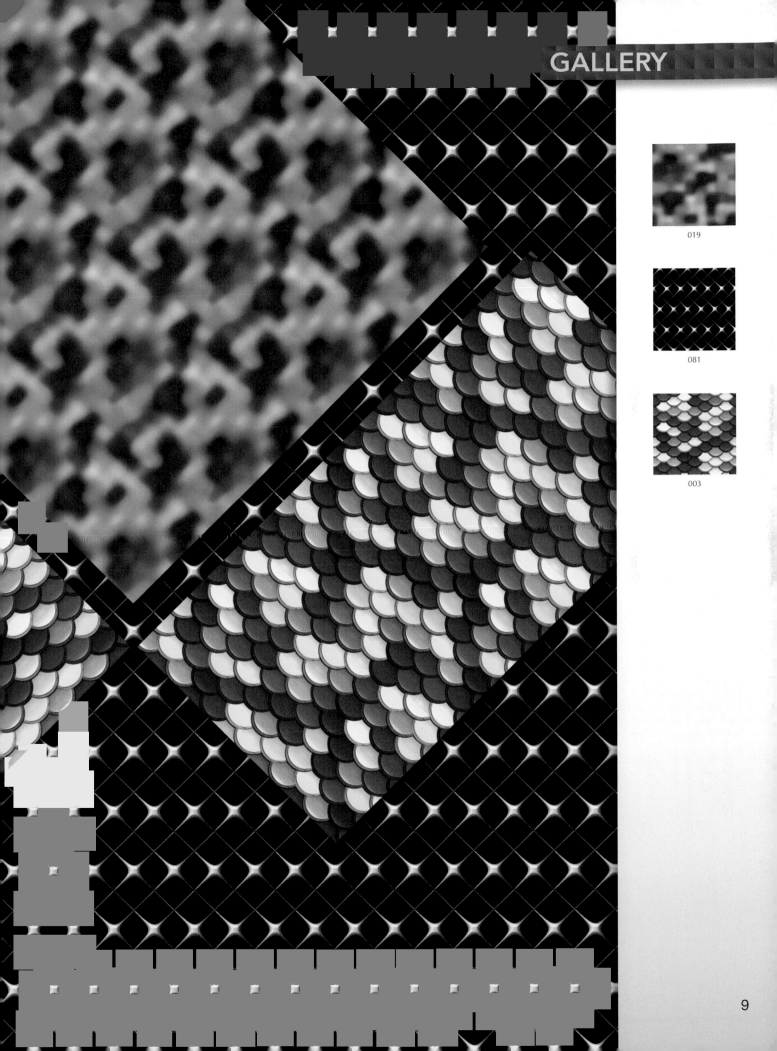

019

081

003

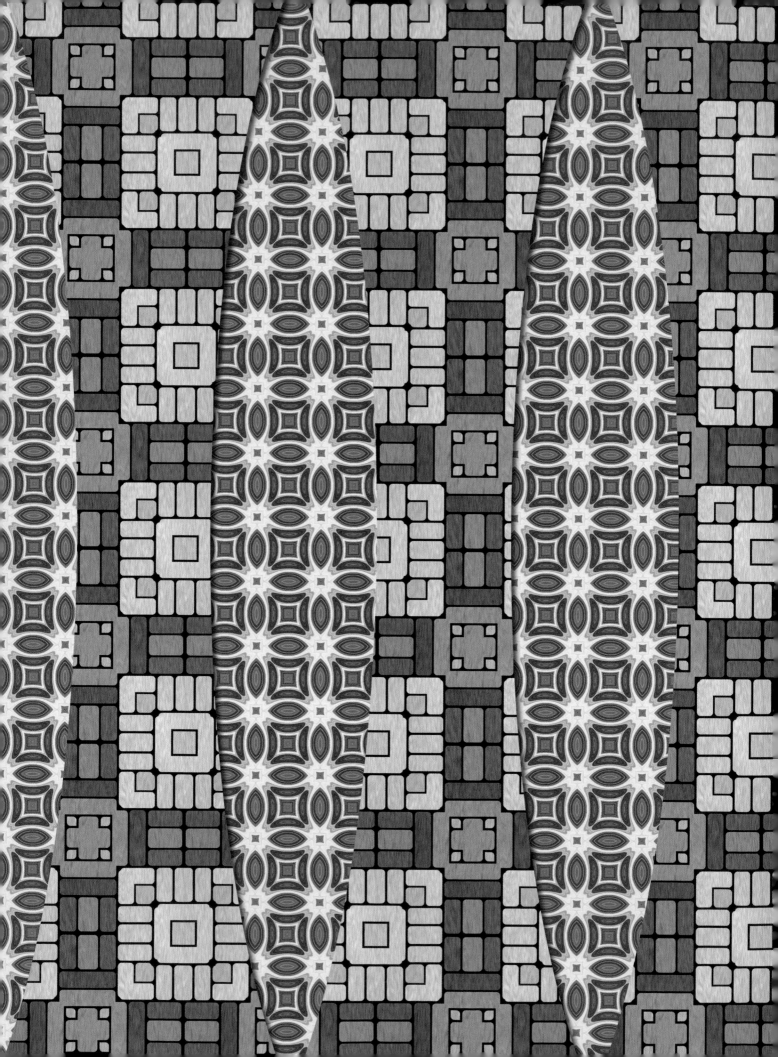

007

149

163

134

046

154

011

024

170

129

098

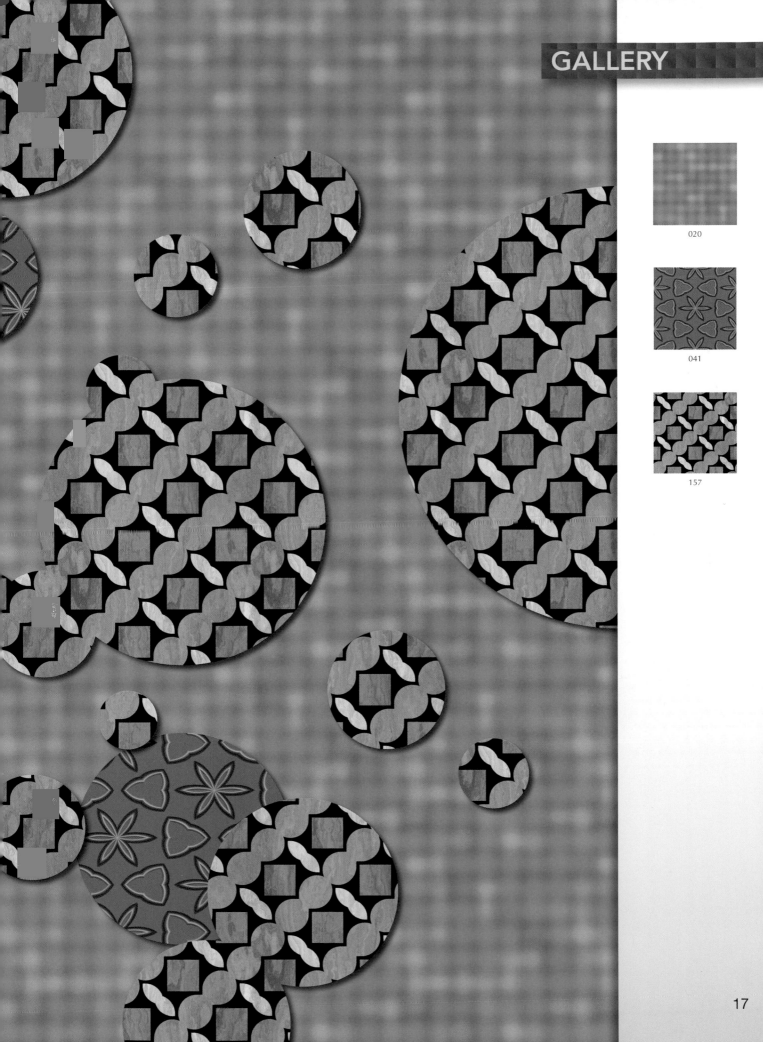

020

041

157

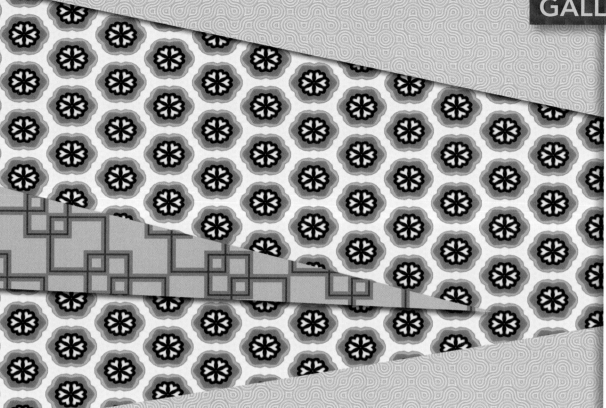

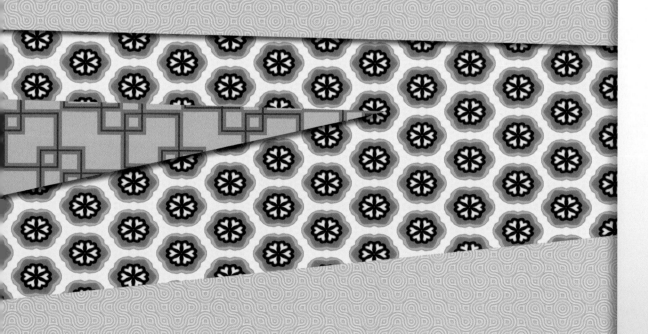

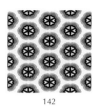

142

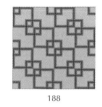

188

102

133

189

005

091

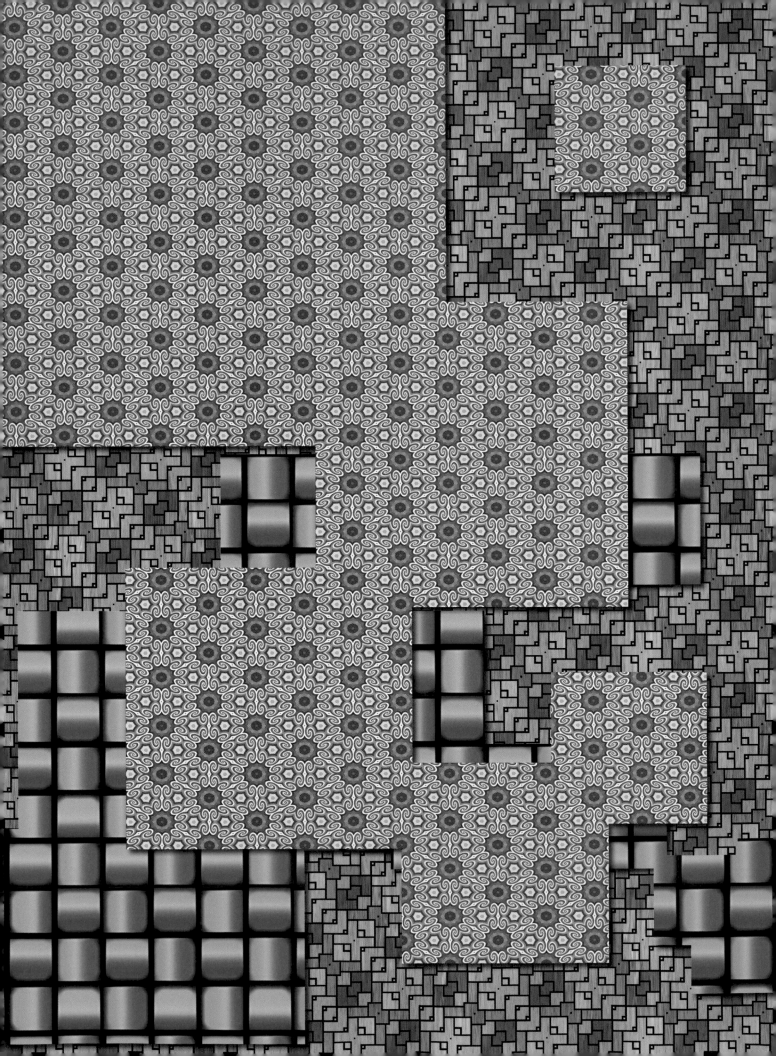

153

014

047

090

034

069

051

004

022

145

159

183

169

055

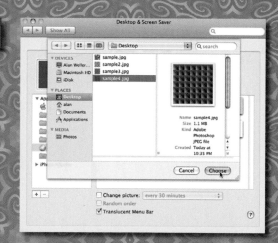

Desktop Pattern for Mac.

1 Choose Apple > System Preferences.

2 From System Preferences Menu choose Desktop & Screen Saver.

3 In the Desktop & Screen Saver Menu be sure to click "Desktop" from the Desktop/Screen Saver button at top.

Then click the plus sign found in lower left corner.

4 Locate the image from the pop-up menu; then click the Choose button.

5 Then choose Tile from the pop-up selector located above the images.

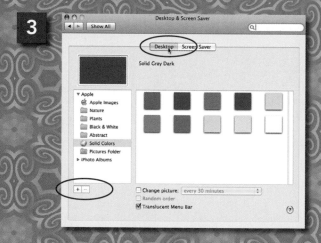

1

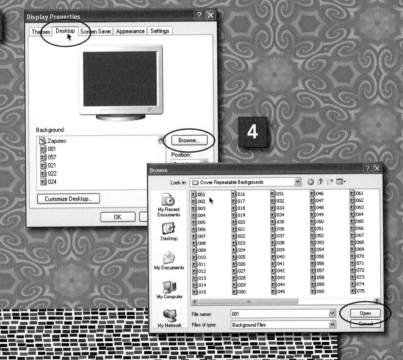

Desktop Pattern for Windows.

1. Choose Start > Control Panel.

2. From the Control Panel Menu choose Display.

3. In the Display Properties Menu choose "Desktop" from the list of items at top.

   Then click the Browse Button.

4. In the Browse Menu find and select the image for the desktop pattern; then click the Open Button.

5. Back In the Display Properties Menu find your image in the "Backgrounds List," select it, then choose "Tile" from the Position Drop-down Menu. Finally, click the Apply Button, then the OK Button.

2

3

4

5

Creating a background pattern.

1 Create a new file or open a working one.

2 Choose Modify > Page Properties.

3 In the Page Properties Dialog box either type in a path to an image or click the Browse button to locate the image you are using to make a pattern.

Note: Use the Web Ready images provided on the CD. These images are 72 dpi and optimized for internet use.

4 Then choose repeat from the Repeat pop-up menu. Click Apply to preview the pattern (**5**) or choose OK to finish.

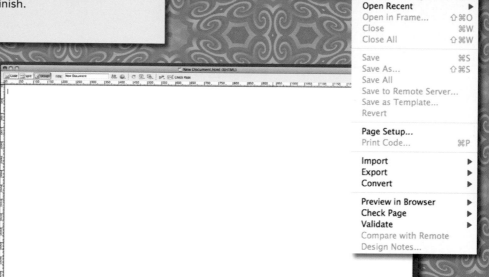

3

Page Properties

Category

- Appearance
- Links
- Headings
- Title/Encoding
- Tracing Image

Appearance

Page font: Default Font **B** *I*

Size: pixels

Text color:

Background color:

Background image: Browse...

Repeat:

Margins

Left: pixels   Right: pixels

Top: pixels   Bottom: pixels

Help   Apply   Cancel   OK

4

Page Properties

Category

- Appearance
- Links
- Headings
- Title/Encoding
- Tracing Image

Appearance

Page font: Default Font **B** *I*

Size: pixels

Text color:

Background color:

Background image: ../../../../dw_sample.jpg   Browse...

Repeat:
- repeat
- repeat-x
- repeat-y
- no-repeat

Margins

Left: pi   Right: pixels

Top: pixels   Bottom: pixels

Help   Apply   Cancel   OK

5

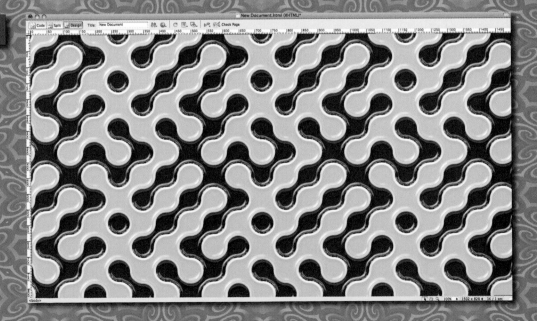

ADOBE ILLUSTRATOR

Turning an image into a fill pattern.

1. Open the file that you want to turn into a fill pattern.
2. Choose Select > All.
3. Choose Edit > Copy.
4. Create a new file or open a working one.
5. Choose Edit > Paste.
6. With the object still selected, Choose Edit > Define Pattern.
7. Enter a name for the pattern in the Pattern Name dialog box.
8. The pattern should show up in the Swatches Menu.

Filling a selection with the pattern.

9. Create a shape to fill with the pattern.
10. Select the shape using the Select Tool from the Tool Bar.
11. Then select the fill pattern from the Swatches Menu. The Highlighted shape should fill with the selected pattern.

5

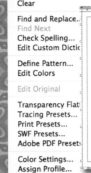

6
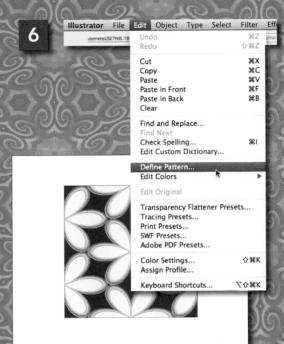

7

8

9

10

11

Making a photoshop image into a pattern.

1. Open the file you want to create a pattern from.

2. Choose Select > All.

3. Choose Edit > Define Pattern.

4. Enter a name for the pattern in the Pattern Name dialog box.

Filling a selection with the pattern.

5. Create a new file or open a working one.

6. Select the layer or part of the image you want to fill.

7. Do one of the following:

   A. Select the Paint Bucket tool In the options bar, choose Pattern from the Fill pop-up menu, and select a pattern from the Pattern pop-up palette. Then click to fill the selected area with the pattern.

   B. Choose Edit > Fill. In the Fill dialog box, for Use, choose Pattern, select a pattern from the pop-up palette, and click OK. If Pattern is dimmed, you need to load a pattern library before you can select this option. (Not Illustrated)

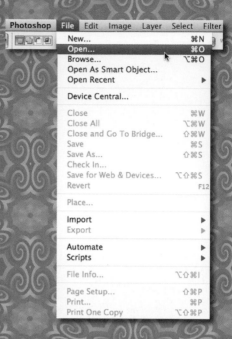

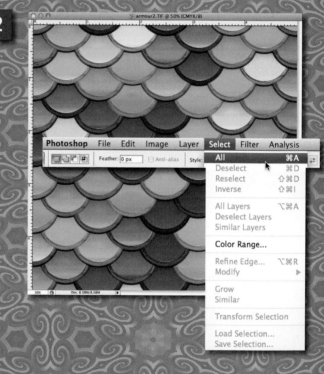

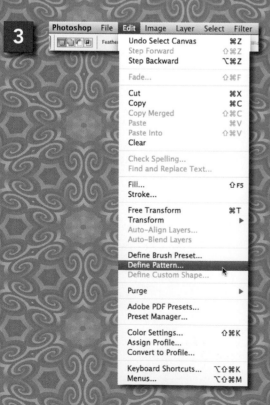

5

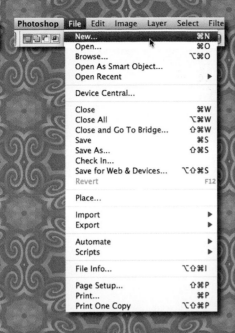

Photoshop File Edit Image Layer Select Filte

New...	⌘N
Open...	⌘O
Browse...	⌥⌘O
Open As Smart Object...	
Open Recent	▶
Device Central...	
Close	⌘W
Close All	⌥⌘W
Close and Go To Bridge...	⇧⌘W
Save	⌘S
Save As...	⇧⌘S
Check In...	
Save for Web & Devices...	⌥⇧⌘S
Revert	F12
Place...	
Import	▶
Export	▶
Automate	▶
Scripts	▶
File Info...	⌥⇧⌘I
Page Setup...	⇧⌘P
Print...	⌘P
Print One Copy	⌥⇧⌘P

6

7-A

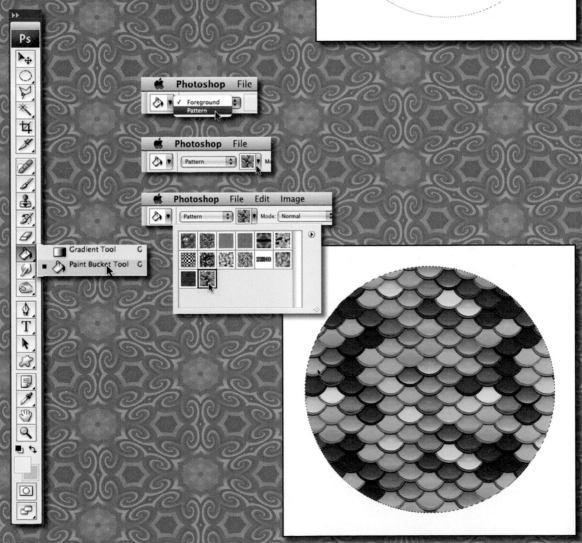

BACKGROUNDS

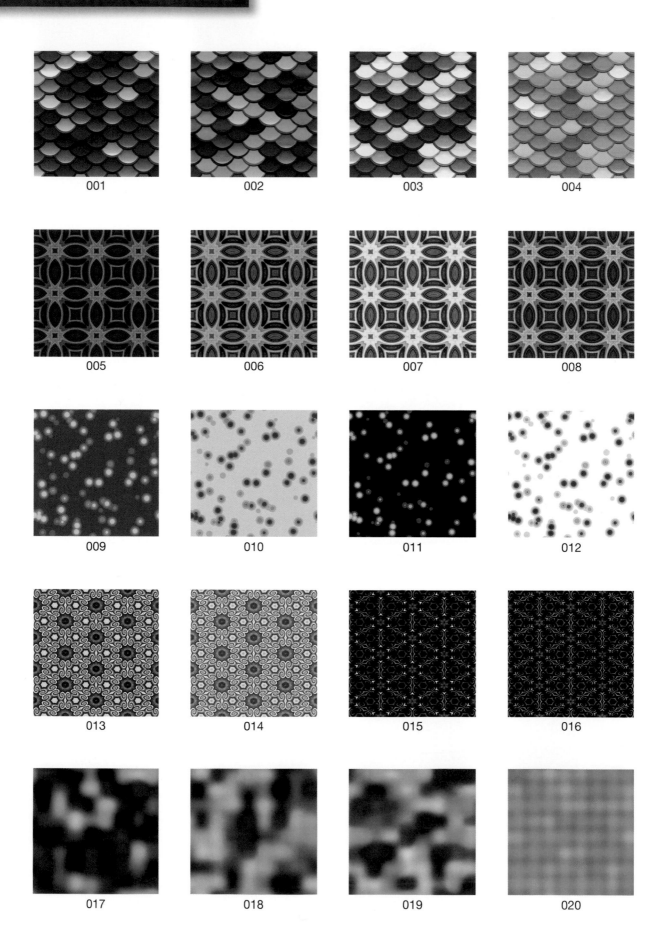

001

002

003

004

005

006

007

008

009

010

011

012

013

014

015

016

017

018

019

020

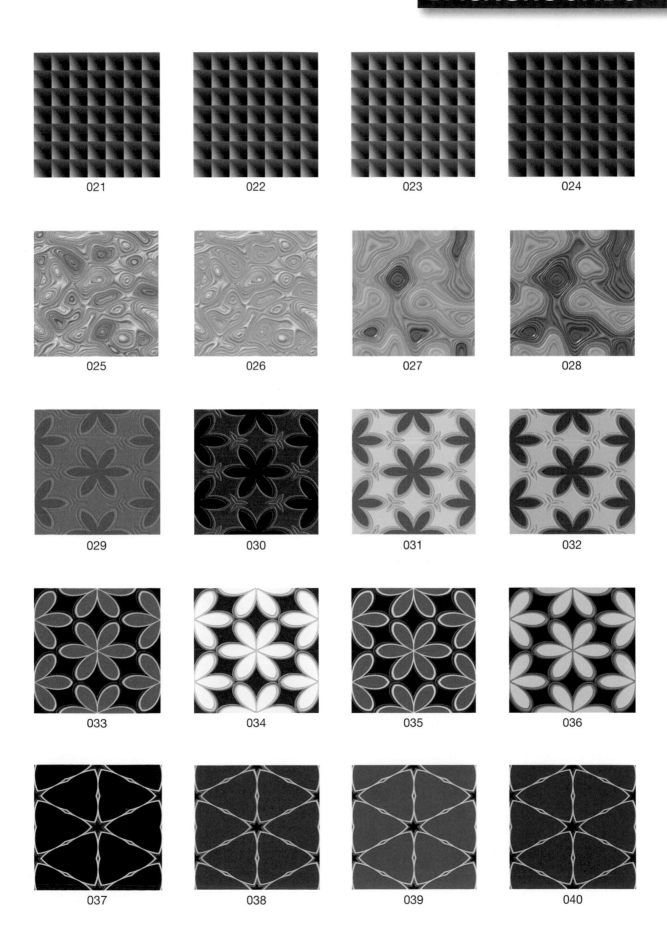

021

022

023

024

025

026

027

028

029

030

031

032

033

034

035

036

037

038

039

040

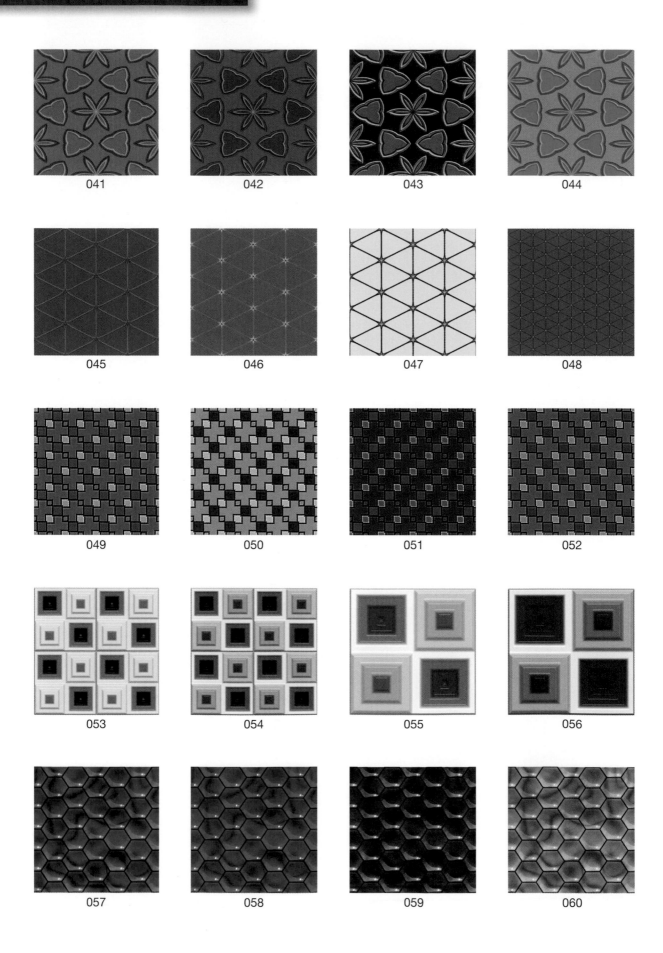

041

042

043

044

045

046

047

048

049

050

051

052

053

054

055

056

057

058

059

060

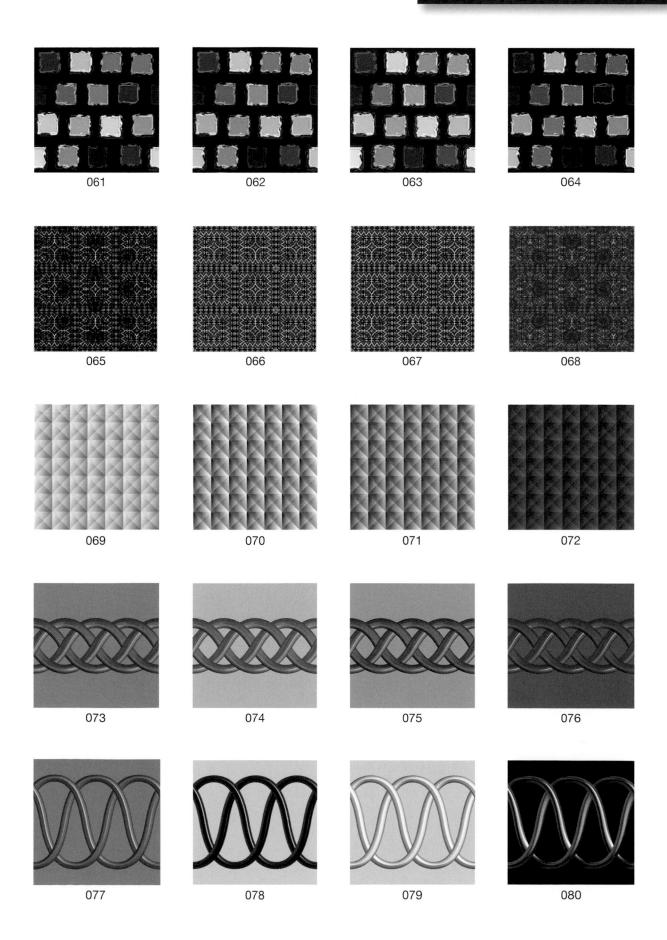

061

062

063

064

065

066

067

068

069

070

071

072

073

074

075

076

077

078

079

080

BACKGROUNDS

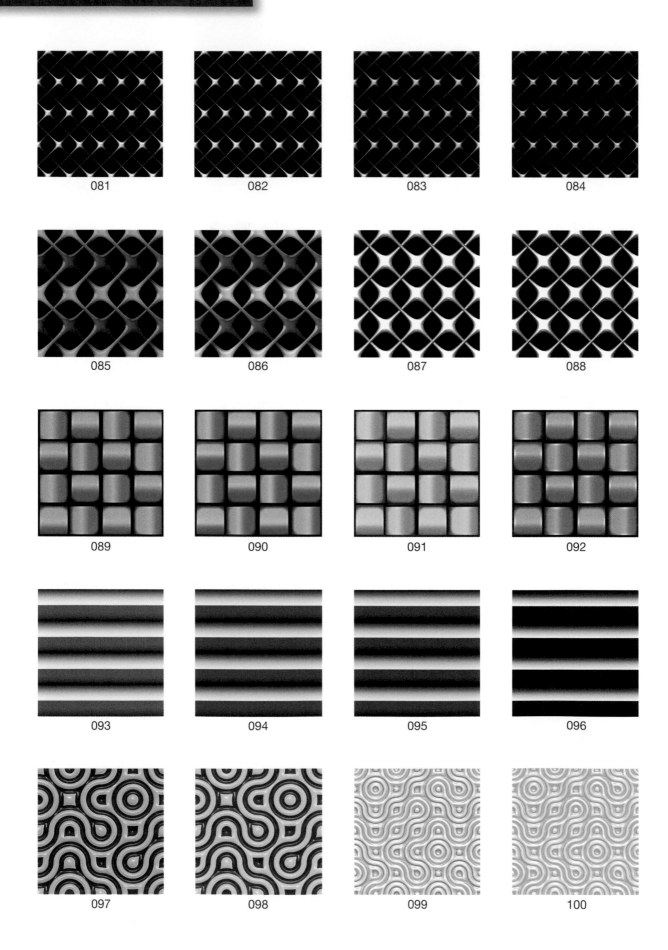

081

082

083

084

085

086

087

088

089

090

091

092

093

094

095

096

097

098

099

100

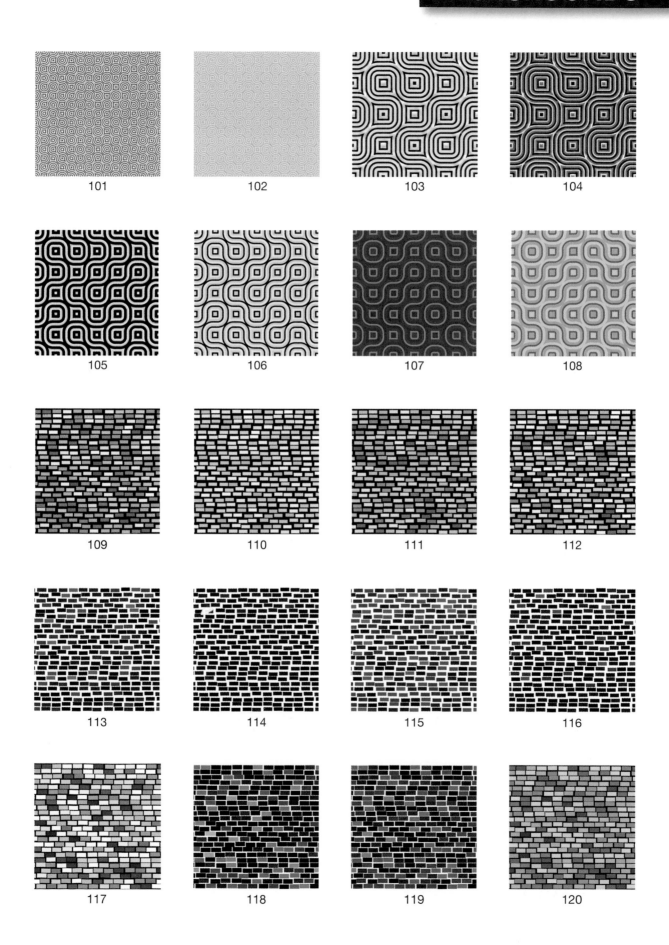

101 102 103 104

105 106 107 108

109 110 111 112

113 114 115 116

117 118 119 120

BACKGROUNDS

121

122

123

124

125

126

127

128

129

130

131

132

133

134

135

136

137

138

139

140

44

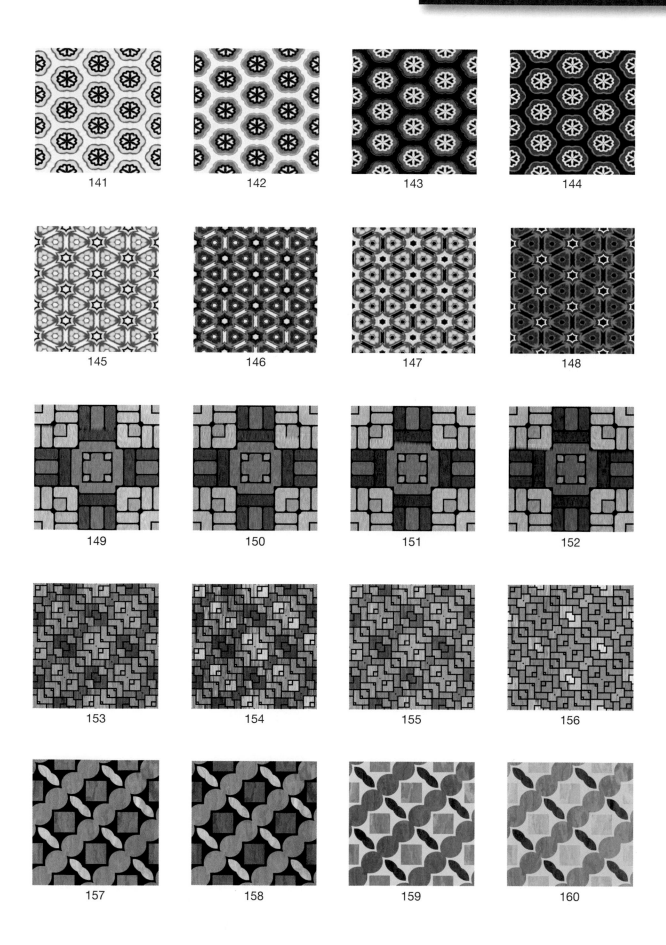

141

142

143

144

145

146

147

148

149

150

151

152

153

154

155

156

157

158

159

160

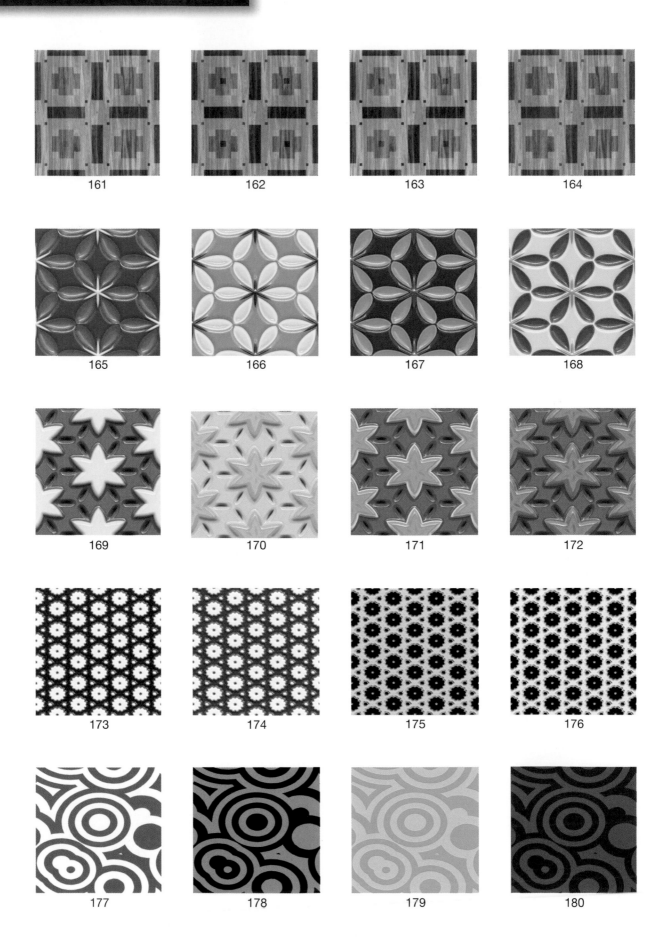

161

162

163

164

165

166

167

168

169

170

171

172

173

174

175

176

177

178

179

180

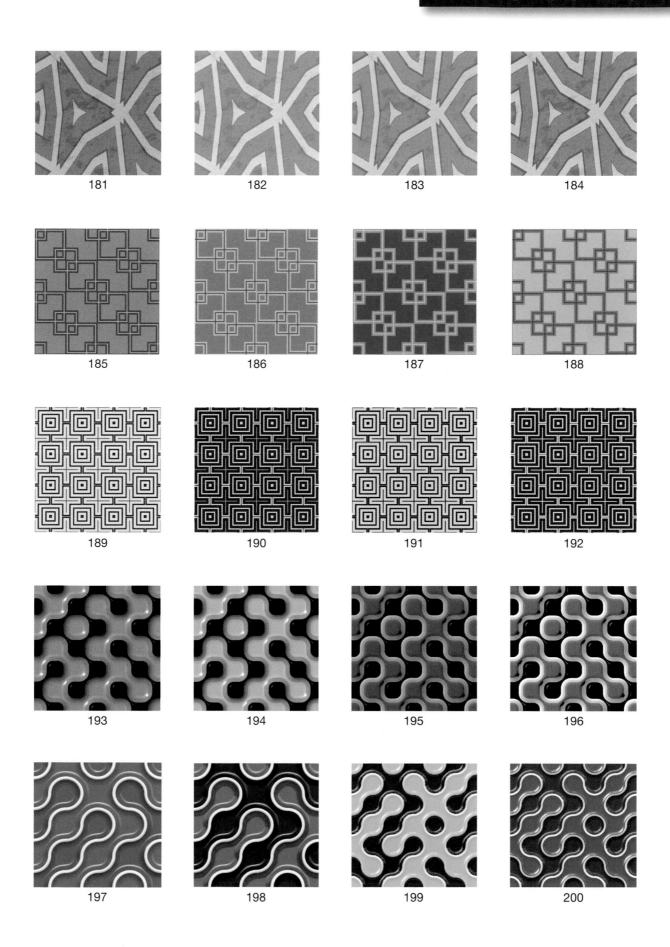

181

182

183

184

185

186

187

188

189

190

191

192

193

194

195

196

197

198

199

200